T0005270

Sometimes We Feel Lonely

By Simone Braxton

Cavendish Square

New York

Published in 2022 by Cavendish Square Publishing, LLC
243 5th Avenue, Suite 136, New York, NY 10016

Copyright © 2022 by Cavendish Square Publishing, LLC

First Edition

This publication represents the opinions and views of the author based on his or her personal experience, knowledge, and research. The information in this book serves as a general guide only. The author and publisher have used their best efforts in preparing this book and disclaim liability rising directly or indirectly from the use and application of this book.

All websites were available and accurate when this book was sent to press.

Library of Congress Cataloging-in-Publication Data

Names: Braxton, Simone, author.
Title: Sometimes we feel lonely / Simone Braxton.
Description: New York : Cavendish Square Publishing, [2022] | Series: Dealing with your feelings | Includes index.
Identifiers: LCCN 2020030635 | ISBN 9781502659927 (library binding) | ISBN 9781502659903 (paperback) | ISBN 9781502659910 (set) | ISBN 9781502659934 (ebook)
Subjects: LCSH: Loneliness in children–Juvenile literature. | Loneliness–Juvenile literature.
Classification: LCC BF723.L64 N37 2022 | DDC 155.4/124–dc23
LC record available at https://lccn.loc.gov/2020030635

Editor: Caitie McAneney
Designer: Deanna Paternostro

The photographs in this book are used by permission and through the courtesy of: Cover Africa Studio/Shutterstock.com; p. 5 Blend Images - JGI/Jamie Grill/Getty Images; pp. 7, 11 fizkes/iStock/Getty Images Plus/Getty Images; pp. 9, 17 SDI Productions/E+/Getty Images; p. 13 KatarzynaBialasiewicz/iStock/Getty Images Plus/Getty Images; p. 15 Alistair Berg/DigitalVision/Getty Images; p. 19 Thomas Barwick/DigitalVision/Getty Images; p. 21 fstop123/E+/Getty Images; p. 23 RichLegg/E+/Getty Images.

Some of the images in this book illustrate individuals who are models. The depictions do not imply actual situations or events.

CPSIA compliance information: Batch #CS22CSQ: For further information contact Cavendish Square Publishing LLC, New York, New York, at 1-877-980-4450.

Printed in the United States of America

Find us on

CONTENTS

All Alone

Have you ever felt like you had no one to talk to? Sometimes we have to do things alone. That can make us sad. Loneliness is a feeling of sadness because we're alone.

You might feel lonely when people leave. Your mom might need to go on a work trip. Your best friend might move away. You might not be able to go to school. It can be hard to be alone.

You might feel lonely even when people are around. Maybe you started going to a new school. Maybe you weren't picked for a team. Maybe you feel left out when people are having fun without you.

What Loneliness Looks Like

Loneliness looks a lot like sadness. You might feel down. You might have a frown on your face. You might be quiet. You might put your head down or try to look smaller.

10

Sometimes being shy can make you lonelier. You might be afraid to talk to others. You might **avoid** looking into their eyes. It can be hard to join in.

How to Deal

It's **normal** to feel lonely
sometimes. People are **social**
animals. We're meant to
live and work with others.
However, sometimes we can't
be around others. You can
use certain tools to deal
with feeling lonely.

Are you lonely because you are shy? You might be afraid of talking to others. Take a deep breath. Say hello to someone new. Join a team or club to meet new people. Making friends can make you less lonely.

You might have to be alone
when it's time to sleep
or when others are busy.
Practice being alone. Think
of things that make you feel
good. You can listen to music.
You can read a book.
You can breathe deeply.

Sometimes you might feel lonely because your friends or family aren't around. You can call them. You can write them letters. You can **video chat**. You can also make new friends.

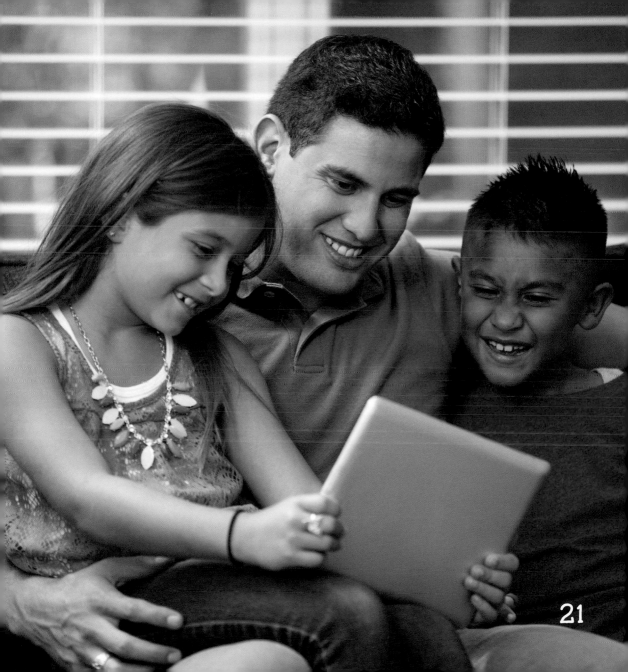

Being alone can make you feel sad. It's important to talk to someone when you feel sad for a long time. Opening up to someone can make you feel better!

WORDS TO KNOW

avoid: To keep away from something.

normal: Usual.

social: Tending to be with others.

video chat: To talk to someone over video.

INDEX